What Is Juneteenth?

by Kirsti Jewel

illustrated by Manuel Gutierrez

Penguin Workshop

For Kwame, Rayshaun, Mila, and
all of my former students—KJ

PENGUIN WORKSHOP
An imprint of Penguin Random House LLC, New York

First published in the United States of America by Penguin Workshop,
an imprint of Penguin Random House LLC, New York, 2022

Visit us online at penguinrandomhouse.com.

Library of Congress Control Number: 2021048986

Printed in the United States of America

ISBN 9780593384695 (paperback)   10 9 8 7 6 5 4 3 2 1 WOR
ISBN 9780593384701 (library binding)   10 9 8 7 6 5 4 3 2 1 WOR

Contents

What Is Juneteenth?

June 19, 1865

There'd been whispers throughout Galveston, Texas, that a paper had been signed. A paper granting freedom to all enslaved people across the Southern states. The people of Texas were the last to hear the news that had changed all of the United States.

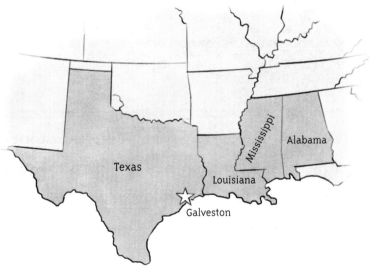

It was 1865, and Black people had suffered under slavery for more than two hundred years. Most Northern states had outlawed slavery by this time. However, in the South, it was legal and white people with money continued to use the forced, unpaid labor of Black people to grow even richer.

Although there are several different stories about what actually happened on June 19, 1865, the one that is most often told says that everyone in town—Black people and the white people who'd enslaved them—were told to gather at Ashton Villa. It had been the headquarters for the Southern army during the Civil War—a war fought for four long years between the Northern and Southern states.

Some Black people at Ashton Villa had hopes that the war might be over. For some time, the North seemed to be winning. Perhaps that explained why there'd been sightings of the US Colored Troops (USCT)—a unit of Black soldiers fighting with the Union army—marching through Galveston. If the North had won the war, what would this mean for Southern states—and, most of all, for Black people? Now Major General Gordon Granger walked onto the balcony overlooking the crowd. He read a handwritten note. Its official name was General Order No. 3, which summarized the famous document known as the Emancipation Proclamation. (To emancipate people means to set them free.)

He said, "The people of Texas are informed that, in accordance with a proclamation from the Executive of the United States [President Abraham Lincoln], all slaves are free."

Free!

As soon as Granger said the word *free*,

Black people cheered and shouted in jubilee—
they were full of joy! Because with one sentence,
Black people learned they were no longer
the property of their white enslavers. The
proclamation recognized them as free human
beings.

People began to dance. Some exclaimed, "Hallelujah!" Others hugged each other and cried. Freedom was a dream that many thought would never come true.

What they didn't know was that the Emancipation Proclamation had been signed on January 1, 1863! It took almost two and a half years for the people of Galveston to find out the news that changed the future of the United States. Why did it take so long for enslaved people in Texas to find out about the Emancipation Proclamation as well as the Union victory two months earlier?

Location was one reason. Among the Confederate states, Texas was farthest west, away from the action of the war. So as Northern troops began winning the war, some enslavers left eastern Southern states such as Louisiana and Alabama and moved to Texas. There they started new plantations (very large farms). They brought along the enslaved people they owned to work their new land.

One formerly enslaved man, named Louis Love, remembered having to leave New Orleans,

Louisiana, suddenly after Northern soldiers took over the city. Love's enslaver knew that if his workers were freed, he'd have to pay them. The very next morning, Love said, that about three hundred enslaved people were ordered onto wagons and moved to Texas.

In Galveston and other parts of Texas, many white people had already heard about the Emancipation Proclamation. However, they purposely kept the news from enslaved people; they wanted to continue having free work for as long as possible.

Tempie Cummins

A formerly enslaved woman named Tempie Cummins always remembered the story her mother told of learning about her freedom. In 1865, Cummins's mother lived in Brookeland, Texas. It is almost two hundred miles from Galveston. One day, she overheard a conversation between the husband and wife who held her in bondage. They weren't going to tell the Black people that they were free until after another crop season or two were over! Cummins recalled that when her mother heard that, she slipped out of the chimney corner and cracked her heels together four times, shouting, "I's free, I's free." Then she ran to the field and told all the other enslaved people, and they quit work.

That was the end of slavery on one plantation!

Also, there hadn't been many Union soldiers in Texas to let Black people know about the Emancipation Proclamation. Even after General Granger made his announcement in Galveston, there were other cities in Texas where it took even longer to hear the news.

June 19, 1865, would soon become a holiday celebrated by all Black Americans across Texas and the South. Decades later, it would be honored across the country. A day of jubilee, as it was often called, for all Americans. A holiday named by blending the words "June" and "nineteenth"—Juneteenth!

CHAPTER 1
Centuries of Slavery

The years of slavery represent a very dark and cruel time in American history. Taken from the western coast of Africa, the first group of African people were brought by ship to Virginia in 1619. Eventually, they were sold at auctions to wealthy white farmers to work on tobacco farms. Slavery existed in all the original thirteen colonies in America. But many years before the Civil War, slavery had been abolished in Northern states.

In the South, Black people were forced for long hours to do backbreaking work—picking cotton and planting tobacco. They cooked and cleaned for their white enslavers and took care of *their* kids, while their own children were also out working the fields.

The Middle Passage

When people were kidnapped from western Africa, they were forced onto ships that made the difficult voyage across the Atlantic Ocean. This voyage is known as the Middle Passage.

The journey was long and grueling, taking many weeks, sometimes months. Ships carried up to six hundred people, chained in extremely tight quarters. There wasn't even enough space to stand up, and so people spent the voyage lying side by

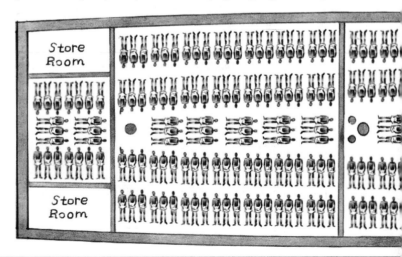

side. They were fed a little water and boiled rice, just barely enough to keep them alive.

Some kidnappers let their captives out onto the deck of the ship for fresh air for short periods of time, but in many cases, the African people spent the entire voyage below deck where it became extremely dirty. People often died from disease and some were killed. In fact, historians say that up to two million people died during the Middle Passage! And if they made it to America, what awaited them was enslavement.

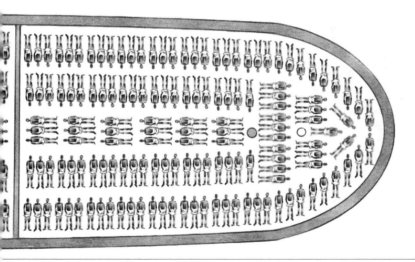

Any children born to enslaved people were automatically enslaved themselves. They were given scraps for food and rags for clothes. They were not allowed to learn to read or write.

What happened if they didn't do as they were told? They were often severely beaten. As punishment, families might be broken up; enslavers would often sell parents or their children to other plantation owners across the South.

People often wonder, "Why didn't enslaved people run away?" Many did! In fact, around one hundred thousand people escaped from slavery. But it was very difficult and dangerous to reach the North. If people were caught, it could result in torture or death.

Auctions of Enslaved People

Before an auction, enslaved people could be held in a private jail for days or weeks. When it was time for them to be auctioned off they'd stand, one after another, on the "auction block." Their strength and other abilities would be described by the auctioneer, and the person was sold to the highest bidder.

Oftentimes, enslaved families were broken apart and sold so quickly, they didn't even have the chance to say goodbye. Family was one of the few things that brought comfort to people during slavery. So, when mothers, or fathers or children, were sold away, it was even more heartbreaking.

When Abraham Lincoln became president in 1861, enslaved people and abolitionists were hopeful. (Abolitionists were people—both white and Black—who fought to end slavery. Many lived in the North.) Lincoln was known for being against slavery. Plantation owners feared that he was going to make owning Black people illegal.

After Abraham Lincoln became president, seven Southern states seceded (this means to separate) from the United States. They formed their own country—the Confederate States of America.

Lincoln said states couldn't do this and war broke out. Then four more Southern states joined the Confederacy. Why didn't these states want to remain in the Union? They wanted to keep slavery. They feared that Lincoln would abolish it.

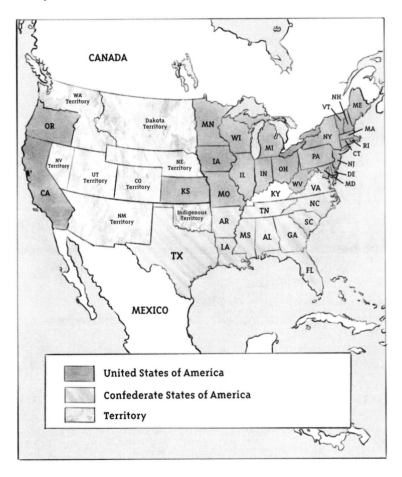

The possibility of becoming free gave Black people in the Confederacy tremendous hope. Lincoln's first step toward universal freedom was the Emancipation Proclamation, issued on January 1, 1863.

Why didn't he use it to free all from bondage?

Lincoln was a practical politician. The border states Kentucky, Delaware, Maryland, Missouri, and West Virginia still allowed slavery.

However, they chose to stay in the Union and didn't join the Confederacy. Lincoln was desperate to keep them from ever seceding. So as not to anger white people in these border states, Lincoln did not free the enslaved people living there. However, all the enslaved people in the Confederacy were suddenly free; they left plantations in great numbers, and many worked for the Union cause, though the living conditions were terrible.

Abraham Lincoln and Slavery

Abraham Lincoln was president from 1861 until 1865. (He was shot and killed by a man loyal to the Confederacy right after the war ended.)

Although Lincoln believed slavery was wrong, he didn't think that Black people were equal to white people. He believed the two races were too different to live together. At one point, Lincoln thought about sending all Black people to a country in Africa called Liberia. However, this idea greatly offended many abolitionists. They said that it was unfair and wrong to send Black people away from a country they helped create. In the end, Lincoln dropped this plan. First came the Emancipation Proclamation, which freed all enslaved people in the Confederacy. Right after the war ended, freedom was granted to all Black people in the United States no matter where they lived.

Horace Greeley, editor of the *New York Daily Tribune*

On August 20, 1862, President Lincoln wrote to an editor of the *New York Daily Tribune*. He stated: "If I could save the Union without freeing any slave I would do it, and if I could save it by freeing all the slaves I would do it . . . What I do about slavery and the colored race, I do because I believe it helps to save this Union."

CHAPTER 2
Fighting for Freedom!

In 1863, with hopes of strengthening his army, President Lincoln allowed Black men to fight for the Union. By the end of the war, around 198,000 Black men served in the military, with 25 winning the Congressional Medal of Honor. Among them was William H. Carney.

William H. Carney

(February 29, 1840–December 9, 1908)

William H. Carney was born in Virginia and spent his childhood enslaved. Along with his family, he moved to Massachusetts, where they were free.

In February 1863, Carney joined the all-Black 54th Massachusetts Infantry Regiment of the Union Army. A month later, he was promoted to sergeant. In July, after a battle his unit lost in South Carolina, Sergeant Carney managed to rescue the Union flag.

He was the first African American to perform a Medal of Honor action, and on March 23, 1900, he received the Medal of Honor for his military service.

Like white women, Black women could not become soldiers. But they made uniforms and blankets for Union soldiers. They were also nurses and spies!

One famous spy was known as Mary Bowser. Bowser kept her true identity unknown by using many aliases. (Aliases are fake names.) Bowser

was a free Black woman who was part of a spy ring led by a white abolitionist named Elizabeth Van Lew. Bowser worked as a servant for Van Lew, but because it was illegal to be Black and free in Virginia, she had to pretend she was enslaved. In order to help the war efforts, Van Lew hired Bowser out as a servant to Jefferson Davis. He was the president of the Confederacy!

Mary Bowser with Jefferson Davis and his wife, Varina

While cleaning Davis's home, Bowser found battle plans and memorized them. Then, she got the information to Van Lew, who passed it along to the Union Army. Women who worked as spies were a huge help in winning the war.

The Union finally won the Civil War on April 9, 1865. However, it would take another two months for the Black people of Texas to learn the news. Now the question to answer was, what would they do with their newfound freedom?

CHAPTER 3
Newly Freed

Among newly freed people, there were some who stayed where they'd been enslaved. Why was that? Well, they understood how to farm the land where they'd lived so many years. Now, they hoped to support themselves by working on it as sharecroppers.

Sharecroppers

Sharecroppers farmed a piece of land that in many cases had once been owned by enslavers. They still didn't own any of the land. In exchange for their labor, sharecroppers were given a place to live—maybe just a shack. They were also given some farming tools and they got to keep part of the crops they grew. It was a very hard life.

Many people considered sharecropping almost like another form of slavery. Still, some sharecroppers were happy to have their independence and no longer be enslaved.

Many other formerly enslaved people left their plantations right away. They wanted to

leave their old life behind. They moved to cities where there might be more job opportunities. Some groups formed their own communities, known as Freedmen's Towns. These towns sprang up across the United States, from New York to California.

Freedmen's Town in Houston, Texas

A lot of Freedmen's Towns were in Texas. Often the first building to go up was a church, then after that, a school. Freedmen's Towns had their own businesses, including grocery stores and barbershops. Besides their belongings, people brought their beloved traditions with them as well. Like Juneteenth.

Some Black people moved to cities and towns to look for lost family members. They went to the state where their loved one had been sent. People put "Have You Seen?" notices in Black newspapers. Many spent years and even decades searching in the hope of being reunited.

On June 14, 1883, a woman named Polly McCray put a notice in a Louisiana newspaper called the *Southwestern Christian Advocate*. It said, "I wish to inquire for my children. Balim was the oldest, Winnie the youngest; Annie came to Texas and is dead; Balim was sold to Gilbert Shivers in Simpson co., Miss., on Silver Creek.

I was sold to his cousin Henry Barry and was brought to Texas by James Oatman. My name when I left there was Polly Shivers. I have not heard or seen them since the war."

Heartbreaking stories like Polly McCray's

explain why celebrating as a family quickly became an important part of Juneteenth traditions. Some would gather near the last place where their relatives had been known to live. Today, family reunions remain an important part of Juneteenth.

CHAPTER 4
Early Celebrations

Juneteenth could've been a day of sadness and regret. In June 1865, some formerly enslaved Texans might have resented being the last to know of their freedom. But Black people chose to make Juneteenth a day of joy.

Starting in 1866, people from across Texas met in Galveston, where Major General Granger first read aloud General Order No. 3. The first documented Juneteenth celebration was held at Reedy Chapel—a church that continues to hold Juneteenth celebrations today. People came in their finest clothes. In the late 1800s, men might wear elegant three-piece suits while women wore long, beautiful gowns. These gowns often had a high neck, and the most expensive ones were trimmed with lace.

Now that they were free, Black people could wear whatever they wanted and be as fancy as they liked. When the holiday first started, families gathered in parks or churches. The Emancipation Proclamation was often read aloud to the crowd.

People sang spirituals that had been sung in the time of slavery. Songs such as "Many Thousands Gone" and "Go Down Moses" were popular during this time.

Spirituals

Music has always been important within the Black community. When the first people were stolen from Africa and put on ships, singing helped captives soothe one another during the terrible voyage.

Years later in the American colonies, themes from the Bible were often part of the songs that became known as spirituals. Slower spirituals about hard times were known as sorrow songs, while upbeat ones expressing joy were called jubilees. There were also songs with secret messages. These coded songs might tell others that there was an opportunity to escape.

For example, in "Swing Low, Sweet Chariot," the "sweet chariot" may have seemed to be about reaching heaven. But when sung on plantations, it was often believed to be code for the Underground Railroad! (The Underground Railroad was not an actual railroad but a system of people and secret locations that helped the enslaved escape bondage.) So spirituals helped many reach freedom.

Parades have also been a big part of Juneteenth. At the first celebrations, Black soldiers who'd fought in the Civil War would ride in front on horses decorated with ribbons. As years passed, the oldest living person who'd once been enslaved was honored. These elders told stories of what their lives had been like. They were celebrated for their wisdom and their strength after having survived such brutality.

One thing is for sure. You can't have Juneteenth without delicious food! In fact, it has become a custom to serve certain foods. What kinds? Strawberries, red velvet cake, watermelon, barbecue, and red punch. You may have noticed that all the foods just listed are deep red.

That isn't a coincidence. The color red represents the bravery and endurance of enslaved people. Red also symbolizes the blood that was shed by Black people in their fight to be free.

Baseball games, fishing, and sometimes rodeos are common Juneteenth activities. At night, fireworks may explode in the sky. Does this make Juneteenth seem like July 4—America's Independence Day? July 4 celebrates Americans declaring freedom from the British. Well, the two holidays are very similar. The biggest difference is that Juneteenth celebrates the day when *everyone* living in America became legally free.

CHAPTER 5
Claiming Space

Long after all Black people were free, often they were still not treated as equals. Even celebrating Juneteenth would soon be a challenge. But do you think this stopped Black people from seeking equality or made them give up Juneteenth?

Absolutely not!

From Galveston, Juneteenth spread to other parts of Texas and then beyond. Yet sometimes white people would kick groups out of public parks or refuse to rent out spaces for their events. However, even if they could only find a tree to gather under, that's where Black people would celebrate Juneteenth.

It had not always been this way. Right after all enslaved people were freed, the United States government granted them some of the same civil rights as white people. This was a period called Reconstruction. Black men could vote and serve in public office. (Two Black men became US senators.) Black people were starting their own businesses. This angered a lot of white people. Then Jim Crow laws were put into place by

the end of the century. This meant that African Americans faced more restrictions on how they lived. This is why it became so difficult to hold events for the day of jubilee.

In 1872, a group of formerly enslaved Black men came together in Houston and made plans to keep Juneteenth alive and well.

Jim Crow Laws

Jim Crow laws were created in the South in the late 1800s to keep non-white people apart from white people. This is called segregation. (To segregate means to separate.) All public places became segregated. There were "Whites Only" restaurants, hotels, schools, public bathrooms— even water fountains. If people of color were allowed in the same building as white people, they had to use a separate entrance. Jim Crow laws were enforced in the South for decades.

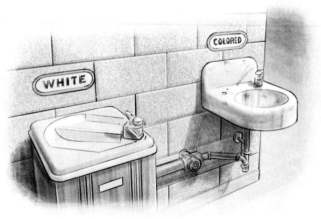

Their names were Reverend Jack Yates, Reverend Elias Dibble, Richard Allen, and Richard Brock. Instead of asking white people to give them space to celebrate Juneteenth, why not purchase their own piece of land? The men pooled their money together—between $800 and $1,000—which was a lot of money back then! With it, they bought ten acres of land in Houston's Third Ward. They named this piece of land Emancipation Park.

Yates, Dibble, Allen, and Brock create Emancipation Park

In Austin, Texas, a formerly enslaved man named Thomas J. White organized a group of businessmen who would work toward owning their own park. They called themselves the Emancipation Park Association. White believed that owning their own land would empower the Black community. In 1907, White and his wife,

Members of the Emancipation Park Association

Mattie B. White, bought five acres of land in East Austin. Like the park located in Houston, it was named Emancipation Park.

Juneteenth celebrations in Austin were celebrated there for thirty years. (Now, they are held in a nearby area known as Rosewood Park.)

About two hours north of Austin, in Mexia, a special organization purchased eighteen acres of land specifically for Juneteenth celebrations. The area is now known as Booker T. Washington Park. Black people had been celebrating their

freedom day there since emancipation. Ralph Long, a Black politician from the community, was known for giving speeches from the back of his wagon to an audience of twenty thousand people.

So, despite Jim Crow laws in the South, Black people found ways for Juneteenth to remain an ever-important part of their history. However, many others chose to leave the places they had always called home and head North, hoping for a better life.

CHAPTER 6
Juneteenth's Migration

Right after the Civil War, 90 percent of all Black Americans lived in the South. But that changed. Over time, Black people from all over the South migrated to (went to live in) other parts of the country.

Where did they go?

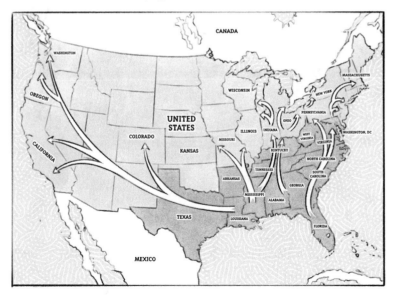

Large Northern cities like Chicago, Detroit, and New York were popular destinations. Many people also migrated to cities in California like Richmond and Los Angeles. The hope was to find better opportunities and escape the racism of the South. From 1916 to 1970, around six million Black people moved from Southern states. This period is called the Great Migration.

A Black family preparing to move North

Although starting a new life in the North, Black southerners brought along their cultural traditions, including soul food, blues music, and cowboy hats (worn by Texans). Through the Great Migration, Juneteenth was also brought to new places across the country. In general, Black Texans moved to the West Coast. It was easier to travel to cities such as San Francisco and Portland, as well as Denver, slightly north, than to East Coast cities. Once one family member settled into a new place, others would follow. Soon there'd be thriving Black communities along the West Coast.

In 1915, a boy named Wesley Johnson Sr. and his mother moved from Beaumont, Texas, to San Francisco, California. Their home was in the Fillmore District where Black Southern

Wesley Johnson Sr.

migrants were quickly creating a community booming with music, art, and delicious food. Later in life, Wesley became a very successful businessman, and in 1945, he organized the Juneteenth celebration on Fillmore Street in San Francisco.

Also in 1945, Clara Peoples brought Juneteenth to Portland, Oregon. Peoples was born in Oklahoma and moved to Portland to work at the shipyards during World War II. (A shipyard is where ships are built.) During World War II, many Black women were able to get these jobs because so many men were off fighting in Europe and the Pacific.

Peoples was surprised to learn that Juneteenth wasn't celebrated in Portland. So she taught her coworkers about Juneteenth and celebrated with them. After years of work, in 1972, Peoples helped organize Portland's first official Juneteenth celebration. By then, she was a beloved community leader, feeding the hungry through her food bank. In 2011, she was officially named "Mother of Juneteenth." Her granddaughter, Jenelle Jack, now leads Portland's Juneteenth celebrations every year.

Clara Peoples with her great-grandaughters

The Great Migration brought Juneteenth to the North and out west where many more Black people came to know about the holiday.

Unfortunately, the better life that migrants had hoped to find was most often out of reach.

CHAPTER 7
A Revival, 1968

In the United States, racism could be found everywhere. There may have not been Jim Crow laws in the North and West, but laws still existed that kept Black people from having the same opportunities as white people. They were often denied a good job, decent housing, and good schools. In the 1950s and 1960s, the country went through major changes. Americans from all backgrounds worked together in the fight for equal rights for Black people. This period is called the civil rights era. It's so significant because of how much real progress was made.

There were waves of peaceful protests. For example, people refused to ride public buses that

Lunch counter sit-in protests

made Black people sit in the back; young Black students sat for hours at lunch counters that only served white people. There were marches like the one in Washington, DC, in 1963 when a very large crowd of 250,000 people demonstrated for fair employment and full equality.

Due to the hard work of Dr. Martin Luther King Jr. and many others, Congress passed the Civil Rights Act in 1964, and President Lyndon B. Johnson signed it. A Voting Rights Act was signed the following year. These two acts got rid of Jim Crow laws, banned segregation in public places such as hotels and restaurants, and ended practices that had kept Black people from voting.

Martin Luther King Jr. at the March on Washington

But during the civil rights era, Juneteenth lost popularity.

Why did this happen?

Historians have a few explanations. Some think that Black people stopped honoring Juneteenth because it focused too much on the past—the time a hundred years earlier when slavery ended. The civil rights movement, on the other hand, was focused on the future and securing the rights

I'm On My

Poor Peoples March on

of Black people. Others say that one goal of the movement was to integrate society—bring people of all colors together. In their opinion, Juneteenth segregated Black people in creating a holiday just for them.

But, in June 1968, new life was breathed into Juneteenth. It happened as a result of a civil rights event that didn't go as planned—the Poor People's Campaign.

The Poor People's Campaign was the idea of Dr. Martin Luther King Jr. A large multiracial group of people would march to Washington, DC, again. This time the demand was for more programs that would help all poor communities, people who didn't have enough money for food or a decent place to live. Tragically, before the trip to

Washington could take place, Dr. King died. On April 4, 1968, a white man shot and killed him on the balcony of a motel in Memphis, Tennessee.

Dr. King's death shook the nation. But it didn't stop his plans. His wife, Coretta Scott King, who was also a leader in the movement, and fellow activist Rev. Ralph David Abernathy headed up the Poor People's Campaign. On

May 13, 1968, three thousand people from all racial backgrounds—white, Indigenous, Asian, Latinx, and Black people—set up tents side by side along the National Mall in Washington, DC.

This was at a time when many people were still living separately, based on the color of their skin. The hope was for Congress to pass an Economic Bill of Rights to give poor people a better life. There was also supposed to be a Solidarity March on May 30. But the date was changed at the last minute. The new date was June 19. Juneteenth! The holiday would show that although the emancipation of enslaved people happened more than one hundred years ago, many people of color were still oppressed.

Did people march? Oh yes!

On Juneteenth 1968, more than fifty thousand people joined the Solidarity March. Mrs. King spoke to the huge crowd at the National Mall about the "sickness of racism, the despair of poverty." Unfortunately, Congress did not pass an Economic Bill of Rights. But not all was lost. It was at the march that many people first learned about Juneteenth. And so, when people returned home, they brought new interest in the holiday with them. Juneteenth went from just being a celebration of the past to a celebration also honoring the present and focusing on hope for the future. Juneteenth continued to move into new cities across the country. How is it celebrated today?

Well, that depends on where you live.

CHAPTER 8
Celebrations Today

Today in many places across the country, Juneteenth traditions from 1866 continue. Celebrations still often take place at parks. Crowds listen to speeches and march in parades. Games are played and barbecue grills are blazing. The traditional red foods are still enjoyed. After all, does anything taste better than red velvet cake?

But as the culture of Black people in America grows ever richer, there are also new ways to celebrate. "Lift Every Voice and Sing," a song written in 1900 and also known as the Black National Anthem, may be followed by a hip-hop performance. The Pan-African flag with its red, black, and green bands may stand alongside the official Juneteenth flag.

Juneteenth Flag

In 1997, Juneteenth got its own flag, created by Ben Haith, the founder of the National Juneteenth Celebration Foundation. He worked with an artist named Lisa Jeanne Graf to create a meaningful symbol for the holiday.

The flag has a single white star in the center. The star stands for two things. First, it represents Texas, known as the Lone Star State. Second, the star represents the freedom of Black people in all fifty states. Around the star there is a burst meant to look a little like a nova. (A nova is what astronomers call a new star.) The burst symbolizes a new beginning for Black people in Texas. The curve in the middle of the flag represents a new horizon. It signifies that new opportunities lie ahead for Black Americans.

The Juneteenth flag is red, white, and blue, sharing the same colors as the American flag. It's a reminder that those who were enslaved, as well as their descendants, are indeed Americans.

In 2007, "June 19, 1865" was added along the right side of the flag to record that all-important date.

If you're in Fort Worth, Texas, on Juneteenth, you may find yourself at a Miss Juneteenth contest. These contests offer a way for young Black women to learn about their past. Contestants write essays about Black history and bring awareness to causes that are important to them. Winners receive a scholarship to help with the cost of

college. The Miss Juneteenth contest started in Texas; however, you can now find them in cities across the country such as Las Vegas, Tampa, and Milwaukee.

Milwaukee also hosts one of the largest Juneteenth celebrations. It began in 1971. It started with about five hundred participants, and now has grown to include tens of thousands of people. It has always been hosted by the Northcott Neighborhood House, which is a community center. Many cities celebrate Juneteenth on a weekend. Milwaukee, however, insists that the holiday be observed right on June 19—even if it falls on a weekday. The city's festivities take on issues that are important today. Politicians shake hands with attendees and address major concerns of the Black community. It's also been a prime time for registering people to vote for upcoming elections.

In Flint, Michigan, you may find yourself playing a large game of dodgeball or competing in a double Dutch contest. Or perhaps you're part of the annual parade, modeled after the first parades in Texas. Community leaders, entertainers, and

church groups all walk, dance, or ride in cars through Flint's Black neighborhoods. The cochair of Flint's Juneteenth celebration, Paul Herring, explained to a reporter of the *Flint Journal* why he believes Juneteenth continues to be important. He said, "I always say, 'We are the children of those who chose to survive.'"

Raven Anderson remembers celebrating Juneteenth in her hometown of Bastrop, Texas, when she was a child. More than 150 relatives from her mother's side of the family get together to cook for their huge family and just enjoy being together. During the day there's a parade on Main Street, and, in the evening, there's a big dance.

Anderson is proud that Bastrop's festivities always include everyone in town, regardless of race. For more than 150 years, Juneteenth has traveled into cities and towns across the country, a little different, perhaps, in each place and yet the same. It's always a day to take pride in being a Black American.

Then, 2020 came when the United States—indeed, the whole world—changed because of a disease called COVID-19. Yet Juneteenth still took place, even during a nationwide shutdown. How it was celebrated changed, yet its theme of joy remained at its center.

CHAPTER 9
Jubilee in 2020

So what happened in 2020? Maybe the question is, what didn't happen?! In March, the United States shut down to combat COVID-19. Because it is spread from one infected person to others, health organizations said the best way to control new cases was to keep people apart from one another. Millions of Americans stayed at home. Offices, restaurants, movie theaters, and schools closed. For children at home, being "in class" meant connecting with teachers and other students by computer. If people went to public spaces, the safest thing was to wear a mask that covered their nose and mouth.

Because so many businesses could no longer operate, millions of people lost their jobs. They had to worry about how they would have money to pay for rent and food.

In the spring, just as people were trying to make sense of the pandemic, there was more tragedy. In late May, a Black man named George Floyd was stopped by police in Minneapolis. They responded to the accusation that he had used a fake twenty-dollar bill at a store. Police officers forced Floyd to the ground. One of the police officers, Derek Chauvin, killed him by keeping a knee pressed hard on his neck for almost nine minutes as Floyd pleaded for his life, saying he couldn't breathe.

George Floyd

His murder was recorded on a young woman's phone and shared across social media, and quickly there were huge nationwide protests against police killings of George Floyd and other Black people.

Earlier in the year, a Black woman named Breonna Taylor was shot dead by police as she slept in her bed. And a Black man named Ahmaud Arbery was pursued and fatally shot while jogging in Georgia by three white men. These killings were brutal reminders that although slavery was long over, Black people couldn't live their lives free from dangers that white people never had to face. Although the pandemic of 2020 was still raging, the murder of Black people couldn't be ignored. And so, in response, people of all races and backgrounds put on their masks and marched through cities such as Louisville, Minneapolis, Oakland, and Detroit.

Black people fighting for their safety and for fair treatment is not new. So why did this moment feel so different? Well, this time, it seemed like more people—no matter their color—were paying attention. Many parents of all backgrounds were having conversations with their children about the history of racism in this country.

On Juneteenth 2020, protests were still going strong. There was a larger, louder conversation happening about racism. Why was a greater percentage of Black people getting COVID-19

than white people? Were doctors giving the same care to Black people as white people? Juneteenth was getting more attention because while it celebrated freedom, it also raised an important question: Were Black people truly equal in the United States? In Prospect Park in Brooklyn, people of all races used Juneteenth to go on a bike protest in honor of Black Lives Matter. (BLM is an important organization created in 2013 by Opal Tometi, Alicia Garza, and Patrisse Cullors working for racial justice, often through protests that put pressure on the US government.) Meanwhile, only a couple of miles away in Fort

Patrisse Cullors, Alicia Garza, and Opal Tometi

Greene Park, hundreds met with their masks on and enjoyed music. Many attendees had been protesting only days before but now took time to celebrate and focus on joy, like at the earliest Juneteenth gatherings.

Due to the pandemic, many cities such as Denver and Portland held Juneteenth events online. Houston replaced its usual parade with a virtual one. Concerts and readings of the Emancipation Proclamation were enjoyed via a computer in people's homes.

A family might have a barbecue or watch a movie about Black history. It wasn't the same kind of celebration with large groups together in person, but it was still the same important holiday. With new energy directed toward Juneteenth and more attention paid to it, people started to wonder why Juneteenth wasn't a national holiday. In 2020, the governors of Massachusetts, New Jersey, New York, and Virginia made it a state holiday. Companies like Twitter, Nike, and Target gave their employees the day off on Juneteenth for the very first time. If July 4 was a national holiday—a day that recognized *some* Americans' independence—shouldn't there be a holiday for the day that everyone became free?

CHAPTER 10
Officially Juneteenth

Although celebrated since 1866, Juneteenth wasn't recognized by a state government until 1980. Which state do you think was the first to do so? Texas, of course! Al Edwards made it happen. (Edwards served in the Texas House of Representatives from 1978 until his death in 2020.) He introduced a bill in 1979 that he hoped the state government would pass to make Juneteenth official.

Al Edwards

Some people, however, chose not to join

his efforts. A Black minister known for leading huge jubilee celebrations did not help Edwards. He, like many others, didn't think that Texas lawmakers would take the bill seriously.

Also, at the same time that Edwards was working on the Juneteenth bill, others were trying very hard to make Martin Luther King Jr.'s birthday a federal holiday. (A federal holiday means the day is recognized by the US government and all government offices are closed.)

The US government had yet to honor any Black American in this way. Would trying to make both days an official holiday be too distracting? There were worries that the holidays were competing against each other. Edwards, however, believed that both days should and could be honored. Following the spirit of the formerly enslaved, Edwards never gave up. In 1980, Juneteenth became a state holiday in Texas. For all his work, Edwards earned the nickname "Mr. Juneteenth."

Al Edwards with Miss Juneteenth, 1980

Martin Luther King Jr. Holiday (MLK Day)

Martin Luther King Jr. and Coretta Scott King

After Martin Luther King Jr. was killed in 1968, Coretta Scott King worked with lawmakers to make his birthday a holiday recognized by all fifty states. In November 1983, President Ronald Reagan signed a Martin Luther King Jr. Day bill, making it a federal holiday. MLK Day was celebrated in 1986 for the first time as a federal holiday. Still, each state decided whether or not to take part in the holiday. It took until 2000—thirty-two years—before every state joined in recognizing it. (Dr. King's birthday is January 15, but the holiday is always on the third Monday in January.) From then on, all government offices were to close on MLK Day, as well as all public schools.

The day honors the hard work Dr. King did for everyone—not only Black people—in the United States. The hope is that people won't simply take the day off but will get involved with their community—perhaps by working in a neighborhood garden—to help further the cause of service and equality in America.

By 2020, every state except for North Dakota, South Dakota, and Hawaii formally observed Juneteenth in some way. The next step was to make Juneteenth a federal holiday, just as MLK Day and July 4 are. It's fitting that many of the people who led the fight were from Texas. One of those Texans is Opal Lee, a retired teacher who grew up in the cities of Marshall and Fort Worth. Born in 1927, she has wonderful memories of going to the local fairgrounds on Juneteenth with her family.

Opal Lee

Lee understands about people's fight for equality because of her own life. At the age of twelve, Lee and her family bought a house in a mostly white neighborhood. Many of their new neighbors didn't like the Lees moving in.

One night, five hundred white people threw rocks and set her family's home on fire. No arrests were made but, of course, this had a huge impact on Opal Lee. Lee has dedicated her life to serving people as both a teacher and a Juneteenth activist. In 2016, at the age of eighty-nine, Lee walked from her home in Fort Worth to Washington, DC—that's 1,402 miles!

She did this to bring attention to Juneteenth and her goal of making it a federal holiday. Each day, she walked two and a half miles to symbolize the two and a half years it took for the news of emancipation to reach enslaved Black people in Galveston.

Another supporter determined to make Juneteenth a national holiday is Texas congresswoman Sheila Jackson Lee. Every year, Jackson Lee tried to get Congress to pass a bill that would make Juneteenth a federal holiday.

The bill is called the Juneteenth National Independence Day Act, and as of 2020 it was supported by more than eighty other members of Congress. In 2020, she told a reporter from *Time* magazine, "One thing

Congresswoman
Sheila Jackson Lee

about national holidays, they help educate people about what the story is." What Lee means is that more will learn about Juneteenth and its importance to all Americans. In 2021, all the hard work of Congresswoman Jackson Lee, Ms. Opal Lee, and many others paid off. On June 17, 2021, President Joe Biden signed the Juneteenth National Independence Day Act, making Juneteenth a federal holiday! The act was effective immediately, making Juneteenth 2021 the first year it was a national holiday.

How will you celebrate Juneteenth this year?

Timeline of Juneteenth

1619 — First enslaved Africans brought to Virginia

1860 — South Carolina secedes from the United States

1861 — Ten other states secede

1863 — President Lincoln signs the Emancipation Proclamation

1865 — The Union Army wins the Civil War

— General Gordon Granger reads General Order No. 3 in Galveston, Texas

1866 — The first Juneteenth is celebrated

1872 — Three businessmen purchase land that becomes Emancipation Park in Houston

1916 — The Great Migration begins

1941 — The United States enters World War II

1968 — Dr. Martin Luther King Jr. is assassinated

— On June 19, fifty thousand people gather for the Solidarity March in Washington, DC

1980 — Juneteenth becomes a state holiday in Texas

1997 — Juneteenth gets its own flag

2013 — Black Lives Matter Movement is started

2016 — Opal Lee walks from Fort Worth, TX, to Washington, DC

2020 — Americans of all races protest police brutality against Black people

2021 — Juneteenth becomes a federal holiday

Timeline of the World

1848 — The Treaty of Guadalupe Hidalgo is signed and the Mexican-American War ends

1860 — The Pony Express begins

1861 — Abraham Lincoln becomes president

1900 — "Lift Every Voice and Sing" is first performed in public

1920 — Harlem Renaissance blossoms throughout New York City

1939 — Billie Holiday records "Strange Fruit"

1957 — Ghana becomes independent from British rule

1961 — President Barack Obama is born in Hawaii

1964 — The Civil Rights Act is passed

1968 — The Montreal Congress of Black Writers Conference takes place

1984 — The first *Dragon Ball* manga is released in Japan

1996 — The Women's National Basketball Association (WNBA) is founded

2013 — Nelson Mandela, South African activist and president, dies at the age of ninety-five

2018 — President Sahle-Work Zewde becomes the first woman president of Ethiopia

2020 — The COVID-19 pandemic strikes

Bibliography

*Books for young readers

Berry, Daina Ramey, and Kali Nicole Gross. *A Black Women's History of the United States*. Boston: Beacon Press, 2020.

*Cooper, Floyd. *Juneteenth for Mazie*. North Mankato, MN: Capstone Young Readers, 2015.

Gordom-Reed, Annette. *On Juneteenth*. New York: Liveright Publishing Corporation, 2021.

*Johnson, Angela, and E. B. Lewis. *All Different Now: Juneteenth, The First Day of Freedom*. New York: Simon & Schuster Books for Young Readers, 2014.

*Wesley, Valerie, and Sharon Wilson. *Freedom's Gifts: A Juneteenth Story*. New York: Simon & Schuster Books for Young Readers, 1997.

Wilkerson, Isabel. *The Warmth of Other Suns*. New York: Random House, 2010.

Zinn, Howard. *A People's History of the United States*. New York: HarperCollins, 2003.

Juneteenth flag

A Juneteenth celebration in Philadelphia, Pennsylvania, 2018

A Juneteenth parade float in Galveston, Texas

Ashton Villa in Galveston, Texas

The Juneteenth Freedom March and Celebration in Seattle, 2020

A stilt walker during a celebration in Philadelphia, Pennsylvania

Performers dance during a Juneteenth celebration in Brooklyn, New York

Mister and Miss Juneteenth during the 2021
celebration in Milwaukee, Wisconsin

A Juneteenth barbecue in Boston, Massachusetts

People look at the original Emancipation Proclamation
at the National Archives Building.

By the President of the United States of America:

A Proclamation.

Whereas, on the twenty-second day of September, in the year of our Lord one thousand eight hundred and sixty-two, a proclamation was issued by the President of the United States, containing, among other things, the following, to wit:

"That on the first day of January, in the
"year of our Lord one thousand eight hundred
"and sixty-three, all persons held as slaves within
"any State or designated part of a State, the people
"whereof shall then be in rebellion against the
"United States, shall be then, thenceforward, and
"forever free; and the Executive Government of the
"United States, including the military and naval
"authority thereof, will recognize and maintain
"the freedom of such persons, and will do no act
"or acts to repress such persons, or any of them,
"in any efforts they may make for their actual
"freedom.
          "That the Executive will, on the first day

First page of the original Emancipation Proclamation

A print of a famous painting showing enslaved people
learning of their emancipation

Two African American sergeants in the Union Army

A game of tug-of-war at a Juneteenth celebration in Riverside, California

Opal Lee, who worked hard to make Juneteenth a federal holiday

A statue of William H. Carney in Norfolk, Virginia

Sheila Jackson Lee, US House representative from Texas

President Joe Biden signs the legislation to make
Juneteenth a federal holiday, in 2021